Soccer Counts!

Barbara Barbieri McGrath and Peter Alderman

Illustrated by Pau Estrada

Charlesbridge

Count on soccer for action and fun.

Come join your friends to kick, pass, and run!

0 Zero

It's zero to zero. You need goals to win.
When everyone's ready, we can begin!

No one knows for sure when soccer was first played. Some people believe soccer has been around for 3,000 years. That's a long time! Soccer was part of the first Olympic games in ancient Greece—but those matches had 27 men on each team, instead of 11 as they do today. The teams played so rough that many players were hurt during the game. Ouch! Today soccer is the world's most popular sport.

1 One

One ball is waiting. The whistle then blows.
Time for the kickoff—then everyone goes!

*The first soccer ball was actually a pig's bladder. It was inflated by
blowing into an opening at the top and knotting it like a balloon. It was
shaped like a big egg! Later, shoemakers made a leather case for the ball.
These models looked more like big peaches. Eventually players used a
round rubber ball, which they inflated with a pump.*

*A regulation ball is 27 to 28 inches around. But if you use your
imagination, you can make anything into a usable soccer ball.
In some countries today children tie their shirts together to use as
a soccer ball. What would you use?*

2 Two

Two keepers try hard to stop the ball.
They leap, stretch, and catch—and sometimes fall!

The goalkeeper's job is to stop the ball from going into the net. She can use her entire body to stop the ball, including her hands. After catching the ball, she can throw it, roll it, or kick it back into play.

Goalkeepers have a big advantage in using their hands—other players cannot use their hands when they are on the field. But goalkeeper is also a very hard position to play. Keepers have to stop that little ball from going into that big goal!

3 Three

Officials watch carefully—can you count three?
When the "ref" blows his whistle, don't dare disagree!

In the early days of soccer, there were no referees, or "refs." Fights were settled by team captains. But that was not always the best way. Teams needed referees to make players obey the rules. If players do not obey the calls of the referees, they get a penalty. Today there is one referee who keeps time and makes calls. Two assistant referees look for out-of-bounds balls. Referees are like soccer police.

4 Four

Count flags in the corners. You'll see there are four.
For an out-of-bounds call, the ref lifts one more.

The field is shaped like a big rectangle. At each corner of the rectangle stands a flag. The flags help players and referees see if the ball goes outside the lines of the rectangle. If it does, the ball is out-of-bounds, and the linesman will raise his own flag to show the players that the ball is now out of play.

Five

If a player should happen to fall to the ground,
Five fingers will help him. A good sport is found.

When soccer was first played in England, it was a wild game played by tough guys. It was so rough that the king threatened to send any villagers caught playing the game to prison. Rules, officials, and sportsmanship made the game much more friendly and accepted.

Being a good sport means playing by the rules and respecting your opponent. Helping another player up is a way to show good sportsmanship.

6 Six

Six substitutes wait on the sidelines to play.
If teammates get tired, they'll help them this day.

Players run, run, and run up and down the field. When they get tired or hurt, they may need to come off the field. The players who take their places are called substitutes. Subs are rested and ready to run, run, and run some more!

7 Seven

The half's almost done—seven minutes to go.
The referee looks at his watch so he'll know.

The players run around for 45 minutes. Halftime gives the players a chance to rest and get a drink. Some players eat oranges for quick energy. The coach also uses this time to give players tips for better play in the second half. Make sure you pick up your orange peels when halftime is over.

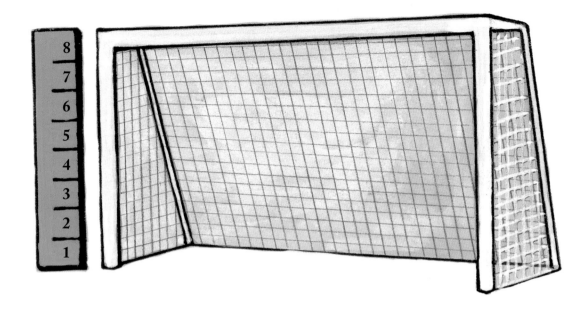

8 Eight

Don't kick the ball too high in the sky.
Remember the goal is just eight feet high.

The goal is eight feet high—about as high as a garage door. Netting at the back stops the ball when a team scores.

Nobody knows what players used for goals in the early days of soccer. They could have used sticks, or lines drawn in the dirt. What would you use if you didn't have a goal?

9 Nine

Controlling the ball is a very hard chore.
This team passes nine times—will they score?

Teams can pass as many times as needed. Players can pass the ball by kicking, heading, or kneeing it in any direction they want. The team that can control the ball and keep possession the longest usually wins the game. Teamwork and good passing are a very important part of the game.

10 Ten

On a free kick, one team stands ten yards from the ball. They line up to block in a long human wall.

Sometimes when a team does something wrong, the other team gets a free kick. That means a player can kick the ball without any of the other team's players nearby. They have to be at least 10 yards away from the kicker. The team that made the mistake, or foul, may have their players stand side by side to try to block the ball after it is kicked. But when the foul happens in the penalty area, the referee awards a penalty kick, and no defensive players can help. Only the keeper can try to stop the ball!

11 Eleven

The half is now over. The teams played their best.
Eleven tired players from each team can rest.

There are 11 players on each team, and four positions: keeper, fullback, halfback, and forward. The keeper protects the goal. The fullbacks are in front of the keeper and defend the goal. Halfbacks help defend the goal and also help score goals. Forwards try to score the goals for the team. A coach can add and take away players from these positions to protect the goal or to score goals.

12 Twelve

The ball's twelve yards out for this penalty kick.
It soars past the keeper…that score was quick!

In soccer a goal counts only if the ball rolls or flies completely over the goal line. "On the line" just isn't good enough! That's why many players try to keep the ball in the air when they boot it toward the goal.

13 Thirteen

This is equipment brought to the game.
Can you count thirteen pieces? Some are the same!

Each player has a shirt with a number on it. They also wear shorts and a pair of socks. A pair of cleats digs into the grass to make it easier to run without slipping. Shin guards protect the players from getting kicked by someone else's cleats. Goalies wear special gloves for handling the ball. Players might also wear a mouth guard to protect their teeth. It's a good idea to bring a ball for practice drills and a water bottle for a drink after all that running!

In some countries, though, soccer equipment is simple—shorts, bare feet, and a ball is all you need to let the fun begin!

14 Fourteen

Fourteen feet scramble. Excitement is high.
The keeper is reaching, but—GOAL! It's a tie!

Players often cluster around the goal when a team is trying to score. They try very hard to kick the ball into the goal. The other team tries just as hard to stop the ball from going into that goal. For every one player, there are two feet. Count the feet. Do you see 14?

15 Fifteen

Fifteen fans cheer. They yell and they shout!
What a great game! But time has run out.

Fans come to watch the game and cheer for their favorite team. Fans can be family, friends, or just people who love watching soccer. Fans make players feel very special by encouraging them.

Two teams shake hands at the end of the game.
The end of the season could bring your team fame!

To Maggie and Kiley, future champions—B. B. M.

With love to my wife Pam and our three sons,
Chris, Shaun, and Jason—P. A.

For Toni, who loves the game—P. E.

Published by Charlesbridge
85 Main Street
Watertown, MA 02472
(617) 926-0329
www.charlesbridge.com

Library of Congress Cataloging-in-Publication Data

McGrath, Barbara Barbieri, 1954–
  Soccer counts! / Barbara Barbieri McGrath and Peter Alderman ;
illustrated by Pau Estrada.
    p. cm.
Summary: An introduction to counting using the history, rules, and fun facts about soccer, the world's most popular game.
  ISBN 1-57091-553-9 (reinforced for library use) — ISBN 1-57091-554-7 (softcover)
  1. Counting—Juvenile literature. 2. Soccer—Juvenile literature. [1. Counting. 2. Soccer.] I. Alderman, Peter. II. Estrada, Pau, ill. III. Title.
  QA113 .M39373 2003
  513.2'11—dc21   2002010489

Printed in South Korea
(hc) 10 9 8 7 6 5 4 3 2 1
(sc) 10 9 8 7 6 5 4 3 2 1

Illustrations done in gouache and ink on Canson paper
Display type set in Quaint ICG and text type set in Adobe Caslon
Color separations, printed and bound by Sung In Printing, South Korea
Production supervision by Brian G. Walker
Designed by Susan Mallory Sherman